The

LABOUR BOLLOCKS

THE ULTIMATE ANTIDOTE TO SPIN

With special glossary to help you talk bollocks and get ahead in Blair's Britain.

ALISTAIR BEATON

POCKET BOOKS

First published in Great Britain by Pocket Books, 2000
An imprint of Simon & Schuster UK Ltd
A Viacom Company

Copyright © Alistair Beaton, 2000

1 3 5 7 9 10 8 6 4 2

Simon & Schuster UK Ltd
Africa House
64-78 Kingsway
London WC2B 6AH

Simon & Schuster Australia
Sydney

A CIP catalogue record for this book is available
from the British Library

ISBN 0-7434-0412-2

Rose illustration © Liane Payne
Printed and bound in Great Britain by
William Clowes Ltd

This little book is dedicated to the memory of the English language, currently in intensive care following a vicious mugging by New Labour spin doctors.

To assist the reader, a comprehensive glossary of New Labour bollocks is included at the back of the book.

WHAT THEY SAID:

Many of Labour's improvements will not
occur overnight.

Labour Party Policy Document, January 2000

WHAT THEY MEANT:

Many of Labour's improvements
will not occur.

WHAT HE SAID:

For better or for worse, we have a democratic
system in this country.
*Lord Falconer, Minister of State in the Cabinet Office,
on* Question Time, *BBC TV, 11 May 2000*

WHAT HE MEANT:

I didn't get where I am today
by being elected.

WHAT HE SAID:

I want to be quite blunt with you about the
modern relationship between today's
Labour Party and the trade unions.
*Tony Blair, Speech to the TGWU Conference,
Blackpool, July 1995*

WHAT HE MEANT:

I've met someone else.

WHAT HE SAID:

Tough on crime and
tough on the
causes of crime.
Jack Straw, hundreds of times

WHAT HE MEANT:

Tough on crime.

WHAT HE SAID:

You can always tell when an election is about to happen. The Tories head straight for the gutter and start playing the race card.

Jack Straw, Shadow Home Secretary,
Speech to Labour Party Conference, October 1996

WHAT HE MEANT:

That's a very nice gutter you've got there.
May I join you?

WHAT HE SAID:

Private prisons are morally repugnant.
Jack Straw, Shadow Home Secretary,
the Independent, *8 March 1995*

WHAT HE MEANT:

Under the Conservatives, private prisons are
morally repugnant.

WHAT HE SAID:

Disorganised railways. And crumbling roads.
That's the legacy the Tories left us.
*John Prescott, Deputy Prime Minister, Speech to Labour
Party Conference, September 1999*

WHAT HE MEANT:

Bugger the railways, let's spend
the money on roads.

WHAT HE SAID:

It's a pity we can't have a
more intelligent debate.
John Prescott, Deputy Prime Minister,
Speech to Labour Party Conference, September 1999

WHAT HE MEANT:

I had to write this speech myself.

WHAT THEY SAID:

Labour aims to achieve a better quality of life
for all by pursuing joined up policies.

Labour Party Policy Document, January 2000

WHAT THEY MEANT:

Tony Blair will be in charge of everything.

WHAT HE SAID:

In 1990-91, under Conservative stewardship, the average number of prisoners held three to a cell designed for one was 2,677. That number has certainly not been exceeded today. The figure is on target for the key performance indicators by which one measures the number of prisoners in overcrowded cells.

Paul Boateng, Minister of State at the Home Office, House of Commons, 17 January 2000

WHAT HE MEANT:

Under New Labour there has been a
threefold increase in key performance
indicators.

WHAT HE SAID:

Last year 67,800 prison places were required.
In 2001-02 we will have 71,400 places.
Paul Boateng, Minister of State at the Home Office,
House of Commons, 17 January 2000

WHAT HE MEANT:

Prison works.

WHAT HE SAID:

We can continue with the over-centralised, secretive and discredited system of government we have at present. Or we can change and trust the people to take more control over their own lives.

Tony Blair,
Speech at Edinburgh University, 28 June 1996

WHAT HE MEANT:

We prefer the former.

WHAT HE SAID:

My vision for the 21st century is of a
popular politics reconciling themes which in
the past have been wrongly regarded as
antagonistic – patriotism and
internationalism; rights and responsibilities;
the promotion of enterprise and the attack
on poverty and discrimination.

The Third Way, New Politics for the New Century,
by Tony Blair, January 1999

WHAT HE MEANT:

I'd quite like to change society
but not if it upsets anyone.

NEW LABOUR TOADIES

No. 1: Mr Ben Bradshaw MP

Is my right hon. Friend [The Prime Minister] aware that, in contrast to what the right hon. Member for Yeovil said, there is widespread delight in the south-west at the extra Government money for schools, including brand new schools in my constituency and in Torridge and West Devon?

Ben Bradshaw,
House of Commons, 22 April 1998

WHAT HE SAID:

Social deprivation should not be seen simply as a matter of money. Children that are brought up in unstable or unhappy families are deprived, irrespective of the wealth of the parents.

Tony Blair, in **What Price a Safe Society?***, April 1994*

WHAT HE MEANT:

Happy families will replace child benefit.

WHAT HE SAID:

Does the hon. Gentleman agree that the Scouts, the Guides, the Boys Brigade and the Duke of Edinburgh's award scheme all have an important role in encouraging young people to participate in the community within a disciplined context?

Paul Boateng,
House of Commons, 5 February 1996

WHAT HE MEANT:

I'm an unspeakable nerd.

WHAT HE SAID:

We have issued fresh guidance to agencies that have to tackle domestic violence, and we have included domestic violence in police best value performance indicators.

Paul Boateng, Minister of State at the Home Office, House of Commons, 10 April 2000

WHAT HE MEANT:

Never let a policeman into your home.

WHAT HE SAID:

No one, least of all me, ever said that our
General Election manifesto was the limit of
our ambitions.
*Tony Blair, Prime Minister, Speech to the Institute of
Public Policy Research, 14 January 1999*

WHAT HE MEANT:

In my second term I plan to abolish death.

WHAT THEY SAID:

In government, Labour will not issue export licences for the sale of arms to regimes that might use them for internal aggression. Nor will we permit the sale of weapons in circumstances where this might intensify or prolong existing armed conflicts or where these weapons might be used to abuse human rights.

The 1997 Labour Manifesto

WHAT THEY MEANT:

Over 50 arms export licences issued to
Indonesia. These include licences for:

- Howitzers, mortars, flame throwers.
- Toxicological agents, riot control agents,
  related equipment.
- Small arms, machine guns, accessories.
- Bombs, torpedoes, rockets, missiles, mines.
- Imaging equipment specially designed
  for military use.

WHAT HE SAID:

Under Labour, Britain is leading Europe...
*Robin Cook, Foreign Secretary, Speech to Labour Party
Conference, September 1999*

WHAT HE MEANT:

Our cows are still madder than theirs.

WHAT HE SAID:

I can authoritatively deny that Labour has any intention of selling the Tote.
Robin Cook, Shadow Foreign Secretary
17 February 1997

WHAT HE MEANT:

My racing tips are famously unreliable.

WHAT HE SAID:

Eight steps towards a
responsible arms trade.

New criteria for the granting of arms export licences.

Announced by the Foreign Secretary,

Robin Cook, 28 July 1997

WHAT HE MEANT:

1. Become Foreign Secretary.

2. Announce that foreign policy is to have ethical dimension.

3. Agree not to block sale of 16 Hawk jets to Indonesia.

4. Ask Gaynor to check out ethical dimensions.

5. Ditch wife.

6. Fly to Indonesia and shake hands with dictator.

7. Make note to stop shooting self in foot.

8. Shoot self in other foot.

WHAT HE SAID:

We are giving London back to Londoners. Next May, Londoners will celebrate by ensuring their next mayor is neither Steven Norris nor Jeffrey Archer.

John Prescott, Deputy Prime Minister, Speech to Labour Party Conference, September 1999

WHAT HE MEANT:

Sometimes, I'm astounded by my own powers of prediction.

WHAT HE SAID:

Our intention is clear. Britain should join a successful single currency, provided the economic conditions are met. It is conditional. It is not inevitable. Both intention and conditions are genuine.

Prime Minister Tony Blair, statement to the House of Commons, 23 February 1999

WHAT HE MEANT:

Our intention is not clear.

WHAT HE SAID:

I do not believe I have done anything wrong or improper. But I should not, with all candour, have entered into the arrangement.

Peter Mandelson, in his letter of resignation, following the revelation that he had borrowed £373,000 from Paymaster General Geoffrey Robinson, 23 December 1998

WHAT HE MEANT:

I didn't think I'd get found out.

WHAT HE SAID:

You try getting change in the public sector and the public services. I bear the scars on my back after two years in government and heaven knows what it will be like after a bit longer.

Tony Blair, Prime Minister, Speech to the British Venture Capital Conference, 6 July 1999

WHAT HE MEANT:

There's always some bastard somewhere who refuses to do exactly as I say.

WHAT HE SAID:

Make no mistake, this government has embarked on a radical shift in the balance of power in this country.

Tony Blair, Prime Minister, Speech to the Institute of Public Policy Research, 14 January 1999

WHAT HE MEANT:

I want to be the Queen.

NEW LABOUR TOADIES

No. 2: Dr Stephen Ladyman MP

I am grateful for that welcome news. I am sure that all Kent MPs will leap to their feet and lavish generous gratitude on the Home Secretary for that answer.

Stephen Ladyman, House of Commons,
10 April 2000

WHAT THEY SAID:

We are putting in place an integrated
transport policy.
Labour Party Policy Document, January 2000

WHAT THEY MEANT:

The trains will meet the buses.
At high speed.
On level crossings.

WHAT THEY SAID:

Labour believes in the interdependence of
town and country.
Labour Party Policy Document, January 2000

WHAT THEY MEANT:

We all have second homes.

WHAT HE SAID:

Our job as a government is not to resist change but to help people through it.

Tony Blair, Prime Minister,
Speech at the annual dinner of the CBI, 17 May 2000

WHAT HE MEANT:

The unemployed will be offered on-line counselling.

NEW LABOUR TOADIES

No. 3: Mrs Diana Organ MP

Does the Prime Minister join me in welcoming the new basis for calculating the unemployment statistics?

Diana Organ, House of Commons, 22 April 1998

WHAT HE SAID:

It is this Government, this New Labour
Government, that has cut capital gains tax
further than ever before.
We have been listening to business.

Tony Blair, Prime Minister,
Speech at the annual dinner of the CBI, 17 May 2000

WHAT HE MEANT:

We have been buggered by business.

WHAT HE SAID:

New Labour does not believe it is
the job of government to interfere in the
running of business.

*Tony Blair, Speech to the Nottingham Chamber of
Commerce, 19 January 1996*

WHAT HE MEANT:

We enjoy being buggered by business.

WHAT HE SAID:

I'm sure he does.

Alastair Campbell, when asked whether the Prime Minister eats GM foods, 15 February 1999

WHAT HE MEANT:

The Prime Minister eats
whatever I tell him to.

WHAT HE SAID:

The jury is out.
Tony Blair, Prime Minister, when asked on
Breakfast with Frost *whether GM foods are safe to eat,*
6 June 1999

WHAT HE MEANT:

Alastair says I don't eat GM foods after all.

WHAT HE SAID:

Working in an unscreened environment in
the single work-focused gateway requires
good security arrangements.

*Andrew Smith, Chief Secretary to the Treasury,
House of Commons, 17 May 2000*

WHAT HE MEANT:

People whose benefits are being taken away
tend to turn a bit nasty.

WHAT HE SAID:

Enterprise should be encouraged through a good climate for business and a tax system which rewards success; and an active welfare state that moves people off benefit and into work.

Tony Blair, Prime Minister, Speech at the annual dinner of the CBI, 17 May 2000

WHAT HE MEANT:

1. Bigger profits for business.
2. Lower taxes for the rich.
3. Abolition of the welfare state.

WHAT HE SAID:

All teachers who are at point 9 on the scale or beyond will be entitled to access the £2,000 uplift and the consequent incremental scales that will take them to £30,000 and beyond. Those who are not yet at point 9 on the scale .... will be entitled ... to access the new fast-track procedures that will enable them to move more rapidly through the existing incremental scale so that they are able to access the new thresholds.

David Blunkett, Minister for Education,
House of Commons, 16 May 2000

WHAT HE MEANT:

I'm giving a few teachers more money.

WHAT HE SAID:

All nurseries receive £1,170, so the playing
field is level in terms of input.

David Blunkett, Minister for Education,
House of Commons, 16 May 2000

WHAT HE MEANT:

I can't speak English properly.

WHAT HE SAID:

We have built prior attainment into the
threshold requirements.
*David Blunkett, Minister for Education, House of
Commons, 16 May 2000*

WHAT HE MEANT:

I still can't speak English properly.

WHAT HE SAID:

With the Objective 1 Status that the Government have obtained for South Yorkshire, it will be possible to ensure that we uplift not only economic activity and employment levels but our communities' aspirations and expectations.

David Blunkett, Minister for Education, House of Commons, 16 May 2000

WHAT HE MEANT:

They'd be dancing in South Yorkshire tonight if only they could work out what the hell I'm talking about.

WHAT HE SAID:

The Tories have dreamt up a new scheme.
They want to flog off the National Air Traffic
Control Service. Labour will do everything to
block this sell-off. Our air is not for sale.
Andrew Smith, Labour Party Conference, October 1996

WHAT HE MEANT:

Our air is for sale.

NEW LABOUR TOADIES

No. 4: Mr Roger Casale MP

Knowing my right hon. Friend's [The Prime Minister's] interest in tennis, I am sure that we shall soon be seeing him in the Labour-held constituency of Wimbledon … While he is there, will he take the time to visit Wimbledon Park, the first school in the constituency where, thanks to the Government's new deal for schools, all the children are already wired up to computers – [Laughter] – and even helping their local Member of Parliament track down the Wombles on the internet?

Roger Casale, House of Commons, 10 June 1998

WHAT THEY SAID:

A fairer system of student grants.
Lifelong Learning, Labour Party policy document, 1996

WHAT THEY MEANT:

No student grants.

WHAT HE SAID:

I will have no truck with a European superstate. If there are moves to create that dragon I will slay it.

Tony Blair, in the Sun, 22 April 1997

WHAT HE MEANT:

I am the patron saint of England.

WHAT HE SAID:

I have always said that our prudence
is for a purpose.

Gordon Brown, Chancellor of the Exchequer,
House of Commons, 21 March 2000

WHAT HE MEANT:

I need cash reserves to provide tax
cuts for the middle classes just
before the next election.

WHAT HE SAID:

Never let anyone say that there is a better place to live than Britain.
Tony Blair, the Daily Express, *3 January 1996*

WHAT HE MEANT:

Personally, I find the food's better in Tuscany.

WHAT HE SAID:

There is a genuine problem with asylum in this country. Unless reasonable and tolerant people deal with what are plain abuses of the system, unreasonable and intolerant people are encouraged.

Tony Blair, Prime Minister,
House of Commons, 22 March 2000

WHAT HE MEANT:

In order to discourage unreasonable and intolerant people, we are going to become unreasonable and intolerant.

WHAT HE SAID:

We need to restore integrity to
our asylum system.

Mike O'Brien,
Parliamentary Under-Secretary of State in the Home
Office, House of Commons, 21 March 2000

WHAT HE MEANT:

We need to keep the bastards out.

WHAT HE SAID:

We believe that it is possible to
create a balance in the immigration
and asylum system.

Mike O'Brien,
Parliamentary Under-Secretary of State in the Home
Office, House of Commons, 22 February 1999

WHAT HE MEANT:

For every refugee we give asylum to, we'll
send one hundred back.

WHAT HE SAID:

We all agree that immigrants have
made an enormous contribution to Britain:
every area of British life has been
enriched by their presence.

Mike O'Brien,
Parliamentary Under-Secretary of State in the Home
Office, House of Commons, 22 February 1999

WHAT HE MEANT:

Thank you and goodnight.

WHAT HE SAID:

Traditional values in a modern setting
should be our guide, not an ideological
argument about public or private enterprise.
*John Prescott, Deputy Prime Minister, speaking to the
Local Government Association, Harrogate, 7 July 1999*

WHAT HE MEANT:

I don't like ideological arguments; Tony
always wins them.

WHAT HE SAID:

How could I be anti-car, driving two Jags?

John Prescott, Deputy Prime Minister,
Speech to Labour Party Conference, September 1999

WHAT HE MEANT:

I am proud of my own small contribution to
the destruction of the environment.

WHAT HE SAID:

We have put the horizon
project back on track.
*Michael Meacher, Environment Minister,
the* Today *programme, BBC Radio, 13 May 2000*

WHAT HE MEANT:

Nobody knows.

WHAT HE SAID:

The minimum wage is a good policy, it's a good principle. .... However, like any decent policy, it has to be sensibly introduced.
Tony Blair, Panorama, BBC TV, 3 October 1994

WHAT HE MEANT:

Around ten pence an hour was
my first thought.

WHAT HE SAID:

Responsibility is what I call the fourth R that
is essential to successful schooling.

Tony Blair,
Speech at University of London, 23 June 1995

WHAT HE MEANT:

The other three are:
Ranting at teachers
Rubbishing schools
Rogering LEA's.

WHAT HE SAID:

I can't stand politicians who wear
God on their sleeves.
Tony Blair, the Sunday Telegraph, *7 April 1996*

WHAT HE MEANT:

I prefer a discreet monogram of
Christ on my Calvin Kleins.

WHAT HE SAID:

Crime and law and order is a much bigger
issue for Labour Party members now as a
result of a larger membership.
Tony Blair, on Walden, *LWT, 26 September 1993*

WHAT HE MEANT:

A lot of Tories have joined our party.

WHAT HE SAID:

The welfare state is one of the great
creations of this century.
The Third Way, New Politics for the New Century,
by Tony Blair, January 1999

WHAT HE MEANT:

And therefore unsuitable for the 21st century.

WHAT HE SAID:

The Third Way stands for a modernised
social democracy, passionate in its
commitment to social justice and the
goals of the centre-left, but flexible,
innovative and forward-looking in the
means to achieve them.

The Third Way, New Politics for the New Century,
by Tony Blair, January 1999

WHAT HE MEANT:

The Third Way stands for [   ] *

*Insert here anything that takes your fancy.

WHAT THEY SAID:

Not wait and see. But prepare and decide.
Labour Party policy document on Europe, 1998,
defining the party's attitude to joining
the single currency

WHAT THEY MEANT:

Prepare to decide to wait and see.

WHAT HE SAID:

We must give our young people a
stake in society but demand good conduct
in return; give chances, but expect them
to be taken, promote opportunity and
obligation together.

Tony Blair, in What Price a Safe Society?, *April 1994*

WHAT HE MEANT:

Do as you're told.

WHAT HE SAID:

We have been elected as New Labour and we
will govern as New Labour.
Tony Blair, Speech to supporters,
morning after election night, 2 May 1997

WHAT HE MEANT:

We have been elected as New Labour and we
will govern as Old Tories.

WHAT HE SAID:

One of the things I like to do, as well as
stimulating more entrepreneurship in the
private sector, is to get a bit of it into the
public sector as well.

Tony Blair, Prime Minister, Speech to the British
Venture Capital Conference, 6 July 1999

WHAT HE MEANT:

I'm asking Walkers Crisps to
fund our schools.

WHAT HE SAID:

Not equal incomes. Not uniform lifestyles or taste or culture. But true equality: equal worth, an equal chance of fulfilment, equal access to knowledge and opportunity.

Tony Blair, Prime Minister, Speech to Labour Party Conference, September 1999

WHAT HE MEANT:

Inequality.

WHAT HE SAID:

A strong civic society takes seriously its
obligations to our elderly.

Gordon Brown, Chancellor of the Exchequer,
House of Commons, 21 March 2000

WHAT HE MEANT:

75p

WHAT HE SAID:

Our Party. New Labour.
Our mission. New Britain.
New Britain. New Labour.
New Britain. New Britain.
Tony Blair, Speech to Labour Conference, October 1994

WHAT HE MEANT:

New Labour.
New Britain.
New Grammar.

WHAT HE SAID:

My project will be complete when the
Labour Party learns to love Peter Mandelson.

Tony Blair,
reported in the Daily Telegraph, *2 March 1996*

WHAT HE MEANT:

I'm quite an ambitious person.

WHAT THEY SAID:

Labour is committed to an open, responsive
democracy held to account by the people.
Labour Party Policy Document, January 2000

WHAT THEY MEANT:

Labour is committed to an open, responsive
democracy held to account by the people.
But not yet.

WHAT THEY SAID:

The country needs a transport system that is safe, efficient, clean and fair.

Labour Party Policy Document, January 2000

WHAT THEY MEANT:

France.

WHAT HE SAID:

Yesterday's stories that I am about to stand as an independent candidate [for London Mayor] are ludicrous. I will not stand against the party I have spent my whole life serving.

Ken Livingstone, the Guardian, 20 February 2000

WHAT HE MEANT:

I'm such a fibber maybe I should apply for a job with Railtrack.

WHAT THEY SAID:

The Rough Sleepers Unit has published a strategy to tackle and prevent rough sleeping.

Labour Party Policy Document, January 2000

WHAT THEY MEANT:

We've bought new mattresses for Labour backbenchers.

WHAT HE SAID:

The Internet is dissolving physical barriers
and levelling the business playing field.

Tony Blair, Prime Minister,
Speech at Knowledge 2000 Conference, 7 March 2000

WHAT HE MEANT:

I sometimes have trouble
with my metaphors.

WHAT HE SAID:

A society without prejudice,
but not without rules.
*Tony Blair, Prime Minister, Speech at Königswinter
Conference, 25 March 2000*

WHAT HE MEANT:

A society where my prejudice rules.

WHAT THEY SAID:

Labour has taken action to
improve rail safety.
Labour Party Policy Document, January 2000

WHAT THEY MEANT:

Labour is building more roads.

WHAT THEY SAID:

We welcome the further impetus that has
been given to the strengthening of European
defence capabilities to enable the European
allies to act more effectively together, thus
reinforcing the transatlantic partnership.

The Washington Declaration, signed by the Heads of
State present at the meeting of NATO in
Washington, DC, 24 April 1999

WHAT THEY MEANT:

More armaments.

WHAT THEY SAID:

We remain determined to stand firm against those who violate human rights, wage war, and conquer territory.

The Washington Declaration, signed by the Heads of State present at the meeting of NATO in Washington, DC, 24 April 1999

WHAT THEY MEANT:

Unless they're bigger than us.
Or too far away.
Or might lose us votes.
Or have no oil.
Or diamonds.
Or might be a good market for our weapons.

What Helen Brinton said:

As I said before, my right hon.
Friend the Minister for the Environment
has taken a superb, excellent and dynamic
lead on the issue.

Helen Brinton, Labour backbencher,
House of Commons, 7 July 1999

What she meant:

I love the Minister for the Environment.

What Helen Brinton said:

I believe that the packages of measures announced in the Budget go a long way to making the car civilised.

Helen Brinton, Labour backbencher, House of Commons, 21 April 1998

What she meant:

I love the Chancellor of the Exchequer.

What Helen Brinton said:

I am glad to join my colleagues who congratulated my right hon. Friend the Deputy Prime Minister on his return from Kyoto, where he undoubtedly played a vital part in brokering the eventual agreement on emissions.

Helen Brinton, Labour backbencher, House of Commons, 15 July 1998

What she meant:

I love the Deputy Prime Minister.

TOP TOADY!

What Helen Brinton said:

I take this opportunity to welcome the
Government's commitment to high-level
political leadership on sustainable
development.

*Helen Brinton, Labour backbencher, House of
Commons, 17 March 1999*

What she meant:

I love the entire Cabinet.

TOP TOADY!

What Helen Brinton said:

Is the Prime Minister aware that one of the first 19 health service walk-in centres opens in my constituency on 10 April? Furthermore, will he take this opportunity to agree that such town and city health centre provision not only helps make health care more accessible but is a very good first step towards reducing health inequality?

Helen Brinton, Labour backbencher, House of Commons, 8 March 2000

What she meant:

But most of all, I love the Prime Minister.

TOP TOADY!

What Helen Brinton said:

I welcome with great happiness the Government's response to the report on housing by the Select Committee on the Environment, Transport and Regional Affairs.

Helen Brinton, House of Commons, 7 December 1998

What she meant:

I don't suppose there's any chance of a job, is there?

NEW LABOUR TOADIES

No. 5: Mr John Hutton MP

Can my right hon. Friend [the Prime Minister] confirm that, in the past 12 months, the Government have given the go-ahead for the construction of 30 new hospitals?...Will my right hon. Friend also confirm that the construction of those new hospitals is not only an excellent way to commemorate the 50th anniversary of the national health service, but provides further evidence that Labour Governments are always good news for the national health service?

John Hutton, House of Commons, 3 June 1998

WHAT HE SAID:

The decision Tony Blair took as a parent had no bearing whatsoever on the politics of the Labour Party. .... It's cheap to make political capital out of the choice of a parent.

Ron Davies, then Shadow Welsh Secretary, BBC Wales, on Tony Blair's decision to send two of his children to the London Oratory School, 3 May 1995

WHAT HE MEANT:

Tony took his decision in a moment of madness.

WHAT HE SAID:

It was a moment of madness.
Former Secretary of State for Wales, Ron Davies,
BBC TV, 30 October 1998

WHAT HE MEANT:

I was trying to find the Care in the
Community hostel on Clapham Common.

WHAT HE SAID:

Let me say this very slowly indeed.
In fact, if you can, watch my lips. No
selection either by examination or interview
under a Labour government.

David Blunkett,
Speech to Labour Conference, October 1995

WHAT HE MEANT:

I was only joking.

WHAT SHE SAID:

Our party's policy remains
opposed to selection.
I support that.
Harriet Harman,
on ITN, on sending her son to a selective grant-
maintained school, 22 January 1996

WHAT SHE MEANT:

I was only joking too.

WHAT HE SAID:

A politician who does not try within their principles to do the best for their child is a politician who is in danger of losing touch with humanity.

Tony Blair, the Daily Mirror, *26 January 1996*

WHAT HE MEANT:

I'm sending my children to a selective school.

WHAT SHE SAID:

We chose St Olave's not because it was selective, but because it was a state school that was right for our son.

Harriet Harman, in the Guardian, 24 January 1996

WHAT SHE MEANT:

We didn't notice St Olave's was a selective school. In fact, we didn't even notice it was a school; we just chose the first building we came across in a nice part of town and by pure chance it turned to be a school and then just imagine our surprise when we discovered it was selective.

WHAT HE SAID:

Let me now refer to the proposal to end the
right of many defendants to elect for trial by
jury ... Surely, cutting down the right to jury
trial, making the system less fair, is not only
wrong but short-sighted and likely to prove
ineffective.

*Jack Straw, as Shadow Home Secretary, on Conservative
proposals to limit the right to trial by jury, House of
Commons, 27 February 1997*

WHAT HE MEANT:

I hope no one will remember I said this
when I come to introduce an almost
identical measure on 7 March 2000.

WHAT THEY SAID:

Labour has shifted up a gear in motoring
policy to tackle congestion hotspots.
Labour Party Policy Document, January 2000

WHAT THEY MEANT:

Put your hand on this metaphor and feel
how hard it is.

WHAT HE SAID:

The crime and disorder reduction partnerships brought into being by the Crime and Disorder Act 1998 published their strategies on 1 April 1999 and are currently implementing them. We recently published a crime reduction strategy, which includes measures to support and develop the partnerships' effectiveness.

Mike O'Brien,
Parliamentary Under-Secretary of State in the Home
Office, House of Commons, 6 December 1999

WHAT HE MEANT:

Hello, I'm Mike. Would you like to come
back to my place for a quick crime and
disorder reduction partnership?

WHAT HE SAID:

After driving back from Wales last night, I parked my car near to my home in south London. I went for a walk on Clapham Common. Whilst walking, I was approached by a man I had never met before who engaged me in conversation. After talking for some minutes he asked me to accompany him and two of his friends to his flat for a meal.

Ron Davies, Secretary of State for Wales, in his letter of resignation, 27 October 1998

WHAT HE MEANT:

Hello, I'm Ron. Is that a crime reduction
strategy you've got in your pocket or are you
just pleased to see me?

WHAT HE SAID:

Under Labour, our air is getting cleaner.
*John Prescott, Deputy Prime Minister, Speech to Labour
Party Conference, September 1999*

WHAT HE MEANT:

Under Labour, our manufacturing industry is
disappearing.

WHAT HE SAID:

Business leaders recognise that what New Labour is saying fits exactly with current thinking in industry.

Tony Blair, Speech in the Assembly Rooms, Derby, 18 January 1996

WHAT HE MEANT:

If it didn't, I wouldn't dare say it.

WHAT HE SAID:

I have visited an estate in Norwich, where a
gang of youths vandalised the shops and the
youth club so badly the council had to
demolish them.

Jack Straw, Shadow Home Secretary,
Speech to Labour Conference, October 1996

WHAT HE MEANT:

Under New Labour the destruction of
communities will be left to market forces.

WHAT HE SAID:

Now what is actually happening is a
process of change whereby we are
going to have One Member
One Vote coming into many,
many of the decisions of the Labour Party.
Tony Blair, on Walden, *LWT, 26 September 1993*

WHAT HE MEANT:

I'm the Member.

WHAT HE SAID:

Labour's commitment to a Freedom of Information Act is clear.

Tony Blair, Speech at the Freedom of Information Awards, London, 25 March 1996

WHAT HE MEANT:

I can't give any further information because under Labour's Freedom of Information Act, information about freedom of information will be excluded from any definition of freedom of information.

NEW LABOUR TOADIES

No. 6: Mr Martin Salter MP

The Minister for Local Government and Housing, Ms Hilary Armstrong: We invited councils to apply for beacon status with the publication last month of the beacon council scheme application brochure. The deadline for applications is 31 July, and we anticipate announcing the first beacon councils in November.

Mr Martin Salter: I thank my right hon. Friend for her reply. Is she aware of the enthusiasm of many forward-looking councils for the beacon council scheme?

WHAT HE SAID:

The values of the Labour Party are good
Scottish values.

Tony Blair, in Scotland on Sunday, 3 March 1996

WHAT HE MEANT:

Rocket salad with porridge.

WHAT HE SAID:

The promotion of equal opportunities does
not imply dull uniformity in welfare
provision and public services.
The Third Way, New Politics for the New Century,
by Tony Blair, January 1999

WHAT HE MEANT:

Welfare provision and public services
will become a zany, unpredictable,
fun experience.

WHAT HE SAID:

Our policies are decided not for tomorrow's newspapers, but for tomorrow's children.
John Prescott, Deputy Prime Minister,
Speech to Labour Party Conference, September 1999

WHAT HE MEANT:

Our policies are decided for tomorrow's newspapers. And sometimes (on a good week) for the Sundays as well.

WHAT HE SAID:

I have no time for the politics of envy.
Tony Blair, Foreword to the 1997 Manifesto

WHAT HE MEANT:

I'm a Tory.

WHAT THEY SAID:

The environment should be as much about improvements to our quality of life at a local level as it is about preventing global environmental destruction.

Labour Party Policy Document, January 2000

WHAT THEY MEANT:

We'll prevent global environmental destruction by planting tulips on roundabouts.

WHAT THEY SAID:

Labour has a vision of a greener future.
Labour Party Policy Document, January 2000

WHAT THEY MEANT:

We hold all our policy meetings at nice hotels in the country.

WHAT HE SAID:

People want honest politics, and they are going to get it.
Tony Blair, during 1997 election campaign, and quoted in House of Commons, 9 July 1997

WHAT HE MEANT:

People want honest politics and they are going to get me.

THE ESSENTIAL BOLLOCKS

A Glossary for Beginners

*LEARN TO TALK BOLLOCKS
AND GET AHEAD IN
NEW LABOUR BRITAIN!*

Bollocks Glossary

ROLLING OUT

Remember, new policies are never just implemented, but rolled out. This implies an ongoing process of great length and effectiveness. It has the added advantage of allowing you to announce the same bit of good news several times over. If you're lucky, you may be able to make the money already committed to the project sound like the allocation of additional funds, but be careful – people have started noticing this.

See also: Putting in place.

LEVEL PLAYING FIELD

Everyone vaguely feels that a level playing field must be a good thing, so nobody's going to be offended when you declare yourself in favour of it. But be careful not to make it sound as if you're in favour of equality – you're not; you're in favour of *equality of opportunity*, which is quite different.

Level playing fields can play havoc with your metaphors, so care is called for. Don't try, for example, to talk about *rolling out our new joined-up threshold requirements across a level playing field*, as it may provoke sniggers in your audience.

BEACONS

Beacons are a vital part of New Labour thinking. Tony Blair set the tone when he declared that he wanted Britain to be *a beacon to the world*, and since then there's been no stopping beacons. Beacon local authorities, beacon schools, beacon hospitals, and so on.

The great thing about beacons is that, by definition, they only apply to a small percentage of any one group of institutions at any one time. This means *beacons don't cost much*. They also get all the other schools, hospitals, councils, etc crazed with feelings of envy and insecurity. This is known as *working in a spirit of healthy competition*.

Bollocks Glossary

NHS DIRECT

A telephone hotline which allows patients to be mis-diagnosed quickly and easily by phone, instead of having to wait for 48 hours on a trolley in a crumbling casualty unit before being mis-diagnosed by an exhausted junior doctor.

Bollocks Glossary

THE THIRD WAY

This usefully vague concept can be used to justify a wide variety of measures, but its essential thrust is to imply that there is no necessary conflict between mutually antagonistic concepts. Thus it becomes possible to call for:

enterprise *and* fairness
globalisation *and* community
patriotism *and* internationalism

This is all bollocks, of course, but if people have a go at you, just smile in a superior way and quote Anthony Giddens at them. Or just make up a Giddens quote. Most people don't actually *read* him.

Bollocks Glossary

CHANGE

This is a key word in the Blair vocabulary. If you want to get ahead in New Labour, you'll need to bang on about *change* as often as possible. It's your job to *help the British people prepare for change*. This means, getting them used to the idea that they're about to be shafted on a daily basis by global capitalism and there isn't anything anyone can do about it. In fact, it's the task of New Labour to facilitate this process, and make Britain a land fit for foreign entrepreneurs to live in.

Bollocks Glossary

PUTTING IN PLACE

New schemes and initiatives can either be *rolled out or put in place*. On balance, putting in place is that little bit more definite, so should be deployed sparingly, in case it gets used against you and somebody finds out that basically you've done fuck all.

The best way of avoiding risk is to use *put in place* together with the title of an initiative which is itself so vague that the combined effect is mildly confusing, e.g., *Fresh Start is being put in place*.

Bollocks Glossary

DIVERSITY

If you want to get ahead in New Labour Britain, it's essential you fully grasp the importance of *diversity*. (Misleadingly, diversity used to be described as *inequality*.) Diversity is a good thing. It can be used to put a positive gloss on the vast differences in income between the rich and the poor, which are of course getting greater under New Labour, but it is also a useful portmanteau word to cover any gross social inequality.

You are also in favour of *ethnic diversity*, but not if this means more asylum seekers.

TARGETING AND FOCUSING

Always, but always, use *target or focus* in preference to *promise*. A target has an aura of scientific precision about it, yet allows a degree of flexibility in delivery that *promise* can never offer. Used as a verb, *target* has an urgent, go-getting quality, which makes it an attractive option. To *target* inner city deprivation is immensely preferable to merely promising to do something about it.

Generally speaking, *focus* is inferior in impact to target, but can be useful where there is obviously no solution (e.g., focusing on pedestrian needs in the age of the car).

Bollocks Glossary

PARTNERSHIP

Become a star of New Labour by talking about *partnership* as much as possible, whether it's partnership between nations or partnership between both sides of industry.

Partnership is important, because the alternative is conflict, and New Labour doesn't like *conflict*. Impress New Labour colleagues by explaining how it's possible to bring about radical change without acknowledging that there are any conflicting interests in society.

Bollocks Glossary

TOUGH

Tough is good. *Tough* shows that you're not a pushover and that you're ready to go out and fight for what you believe. But it's very important you don't take on the wrong opponents. Thus, it's okay to be tough on juvenile crime (*young thugs*), trade unions, bad teachers, and any sad bastard who still believes in socialism. It's NOT okay to be tough on multi-national capital (too powerful), car drivers (too many of them) and China (too big).

MODERNISATION

You are in favour of modernisation. Always.
No exceptions. You can always decide later
what exactly it means.

Modernisation should be used as if it is value-
free, an objective process which cannot be
resisted, especially if it is something highly
contentious, like taking away benefits.
Additional government spending can often
be made conditional upon *modernisation* –
i.e., getting people to do exactly what we
want them to do.

CORE

Traditionally used in the phrase *core values*, which are the eternal Labour values Millbank has decided will play best to the media in any particular week. If you're out meeting the grass roots (though this is best avoided) be sure to emphasise *core values in a modern setting*.

Increasingly, there has been concern about Labour's *core vote*, because nobody can remember where it's gone.

NB: *Core vote* is not an Officially Approved New Labour Phrase, and all use of it should be cleared in advance with party headquarters.

PUBLIC-PRIVATE PARTNERSHIPS

Use *public-private partnerships* rather than
privatisation, which doesn't enjoy the cachet
it once did, possibly due to
a) the high cost of water
b) the almost complete absence of buses
c) the tendency of trains to crash and
kill lots of people.

Emphasise the public part (never, ever, talk
of *private-public partnerships*). Explain that
only the private sector can provide the
investment needed. If anyone asks 'why?'
cough loudly and pretend you've
swallowed a peanut.

THE FORCES OF CONSERVATISM

Almost as flexible a phrase as *The Third Way*, this can be used to describe trade unionists, socialists, civil servants, anarchists, unruly teenagers, demonstrators, teachers, basically, anyone who's unwilling to change in exactly the way Tony Blair wants them to change.

NB: *The forces of Conservatism* should <u>not</u> be used to describe Conservatives.

Bollocks Glossary

AN ACTIVE WELFARE STATE

It is essential that all New Labour Ministers, Special Advisers, and MP's talk about *an active welfare state*. It can be very, very damaging to one's career to talk about *getting rid of the welfare state* (except in private with the Prime Minister).

Be careful not to use capital letters, since this imbues the concept with unwanted significance. Ditto with specific parts of the same. Thus, *national health service*, not *National Health Service*.

Bollocks Glossary

PRUDENCE

Prudence is a close friend of Gordon Brown's. Gordon talks about her a great deal. It's probably best not to follow Gordon's example, otherwise people might find you a bit dull.

SUPER

The word you hope the tabloids will use to describe the tiny minority of teachers, nurses etc to whom you're going to give more money. Hence *Superheads*, *Superteachers*, *Supernurses*, etc, who are paid extra to *turn around* a failing school / class / ward.

Ideally, *Superheads*, *Superteachers* and *Supernurses* should be drawn from a business background, but the public can be a bit sensitive on that issue, so for the foreseeable future it's probably best to select people with at least a nodding acquaintance with their profession.

Bollocks Glossary

EXCELLENCE IN CITIES

An *initiative* which allows selected schools to
employ *Learning Mentors*.
These are non-teaching staff whose job it is
to select and give special help to
a) under-achieving and
b) gifted and talented children.

NB: Do *not* refer to this as 'selection'.

Bollocks Glossary

THE SINGLE WORK FOCUSED GATEWAY

Few people are entirely sure what this is, which is probably why it's been re-named the *One* service. But it's still a very useful phrase to drop into casual conversation since it suggests a familiarity with the mechanics of the Third Way (which nobody entirely understands either).

Essentially, a *single work focused gateway* is a means of forcing benefit claimants to attend interviews with personal advisers, on pain of losing benefit. This compulsion element is officially known as *Full Participation*.

Bollocks Glossary

RIGHTS AND OBLIGATIONS

Never use *rights* without mentioning *obligations* (or conceivably, *duties*, or *responsibilities*) in the same sentence. If you start using *rights* on its own, people could get the idea that rights are somehow automatic and inalienable.

The concept of *human rights* should be used sparingly, and only about people who live in other (preferably small and unimportant) countries.

POVERTY

Do not mention *poverty*. Talk about *social exclusion* instead. The use of the word *poverty* only encourages people to think that it can be dealt with simply, ie by making sure that poor people get more money. This is patently ridiculous.

Social exclusion indicates to the listener or reader the full complexity of the problem, and the near-impossibility of solving it. (Though it is definitely something which New Labour should be seen to be *tackling*.)

Bollocks Glossary

PERFORMANCE

Remember: no rewards without better *performance*. So if you're meeting a bunch of teachers who want more money, tell them they might just get some, but only in return for *improved performance*. If they're already working 16-hour days and look completely shattered, explain they'll just have to do better, otherwise they'll be *rooted out*.

NB: Improved performance in return for higher rewards does not apply to the directors of Railtrack and other privatised utilities.

CONFIDENCE

Getting ahead in the modern Labour Party means being *confident* as a person and believing in *confidence* as an ideal. Tony Blair wants Britain to be a *confident nation*, which means a nation that can push other nations around, like we used to be able to do in the days of Empire, only now the plan is to do it by means of technology and our brilliant knowledge-based economy.

Personal confidence is as important to a Labour politician as *national confidence*. So if the man at the door of The Ivy says there isn't a table available for you, just walk straight past and show the little shit who's boss.

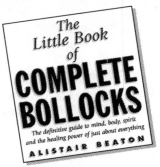

The Little Book of COMPLETE BOLLOCKS

The definitive guide to mind, body, spirit and the healing power of just about everything

ALISTAIR BEATON

The only book in the entire universe that can solve every single problem in your life – for only £2.99

In this witty hatchet job on the therapy culture, writer and broadcaster Alistair Beaton invites you to make friends with your anxiety, give your anger a hug, and have a good long satisfying shag with your negativity.

Price £2.99

ISBN 0 671 03767 6